Pricing Strategy for Laboratory Instruments and the Marketing and Sales Process

William Lipps

Contents

Pricing Strategy for Laboratory Instruments

Pricing Strategy for Laboratory Instruments

Pricing is always a challenging decision particularly in mature markets where there are existing competitors and you are not the market leader. If you are not the market leader all of your products will be compared to the leader.

Pricing is always on value. A manufacturer may do "cost plus" pricing (% margin pricing is typical for product driven business to business marketing), however the purchaser ALWAYS buys on value. The value is not determined by

the instrument manufacturer.   VALUE is
determined by the customer.

What the instrument manufacturer may believe
is valuable may be of no value to a particular
user/market. Also, different markets may
perceive different features to have different
value. One person may believe that a certain
feature is of high value while another sees no
benefit to that feature at all.

Value goes beyond the tangible product. Value
is DEFINED as the extent to which a product or
service helps the customer do more effectively,
conveniently, or affordable a job they've been
trying to do.

Value is quantifiable and is based on outcome
or consequences. The product itself has value,
but there are ALWAYS subjective assessments
(beliefs) that add non quantifiable value. If

there is an unmet need (a new instrument that does a new test), or one technology significantly outperforms "the old way", then the new technology/product becomes the dominant feature/value differentiator.

If certain features provide economic benefits compared to a competitor, and if the benefit is quantifiable and proven. Then the feature that adds the extra value becomes a DIFFERENTIATOR worth a higher price.

In business to business buying you cannot overlook the RISK and career consequences that come together as PSYCHOLOGICAL benefits. "Nobody ever gets fired for buying an Agilent" is an example. Buying Agilent, or the market leader, is considered a safe bet. Psychological value can include:

1. Brand

2. Risk

3. Uncertainty

4. Complexity

5. Relationship and trust

6. Convenience

7. Ease-of-use

8. Hassle of changing to another brand

9. "Look and feel"

10. Sales-force technical knowledge and
    expertise

For example, assume two companies are selling
instruments that cannot be differentiated by
product features. The company perceived, by
the customer, as having the highest expertise
should be able to command the higher price.
The market leader is most often perceived, by
the customer, as having the most expertise.

Other factors to consider in brand replacement include cost per test, and cost compared to other alternatives. You should be able to show that your brand will lower costs, or at least not increase them.

A value matrix positions a mature product in the middle as neutral. Pricing is determined by "fair market value". The price per feature set can be estimated by tabulating the features and the average price of the market leader. To do this, examine several "bids" lost to the market leader and list the competitor's features. These features are what the market has determined has a value of the average price of the winning bids. The average price is the "market value" of an instrument with a feature set the market considers has that value. The price is what the market is willing to pay. The features are what the market wants.

Pricing Strategy for Laboratory Instruments

Tabulate your features and compare to the features the market wants. Are yours equivalent? Are yours more? Or are they less?

The market leader defines the market price and feature set. Place the market leader in the neutral spot on the pricing curve (Figure 1). This curve plots the value versus price. The midpoint is the market price of the product and the feature set is what the market determines is worth the price. If your price was close to that of the market leader and your feature set is similar, then you are losing on brand recognition. If your feature set is better and you still lose, you need to better communicate your benefits, decrease features/benefits, or reduce price to overcome the psychological value (brand recognition) of the competitor.

Pricing Strategy for Laboratory Instruments

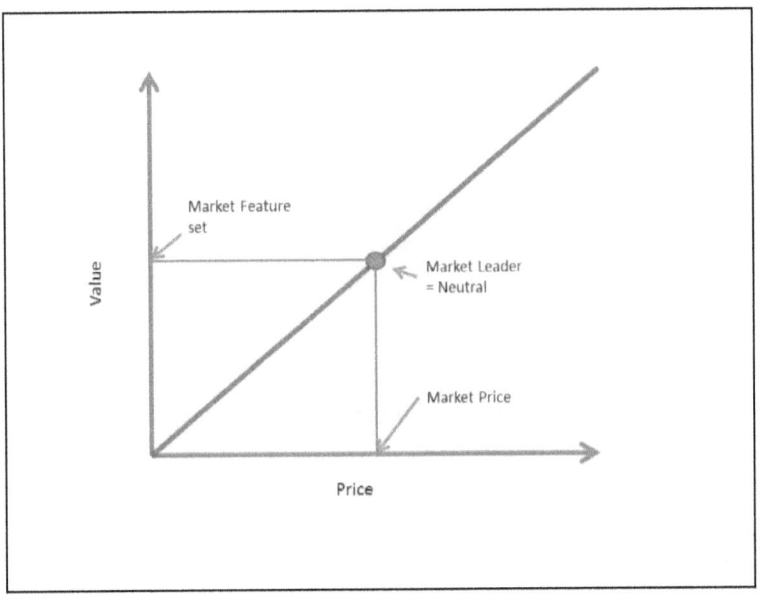

Figure 1 Pricing Curve

Figure 2 plots the market leader in the neutral position and two other bids. One bid (P1) was lower in price than the market leader, and the

other bid (P2) was higher in price than the
market leader. The value (V1) of the low bidder
and the value (V2) of the high bidder are both
PERCEIVED by the customer as lower than the
market leader. If both P1 and P2 are considered
by the respective manufacturer's as having
equivalent VALUE as the market leader, the
difference in price is psychological (due to
brand recognition). If P2 truly has greater
features/benefits to justify the higher price,
then the benefits were poorly communicated.

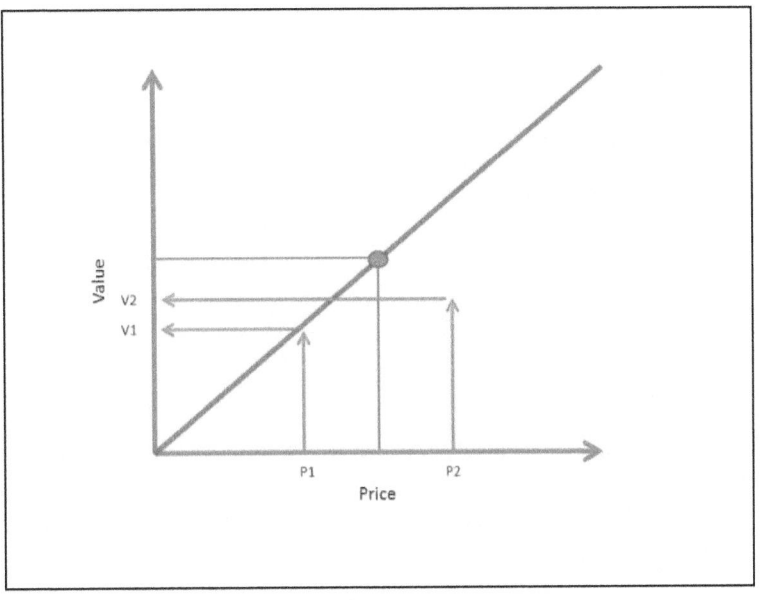

Figure 2 pricing curve with competitive bids

If P1 features are truly equivalent to the market
leader, then P1 should have been the winning
bidder. Losing this bid indicates inability to
overcome brand recognition (or not taking into
account the customer's added psychological
value of brand) or that the benefits/features

11

were not adequately communicated. In general,
a price that falls above the curve should win,
and a price that falls below the line will lose
(Figure 3).

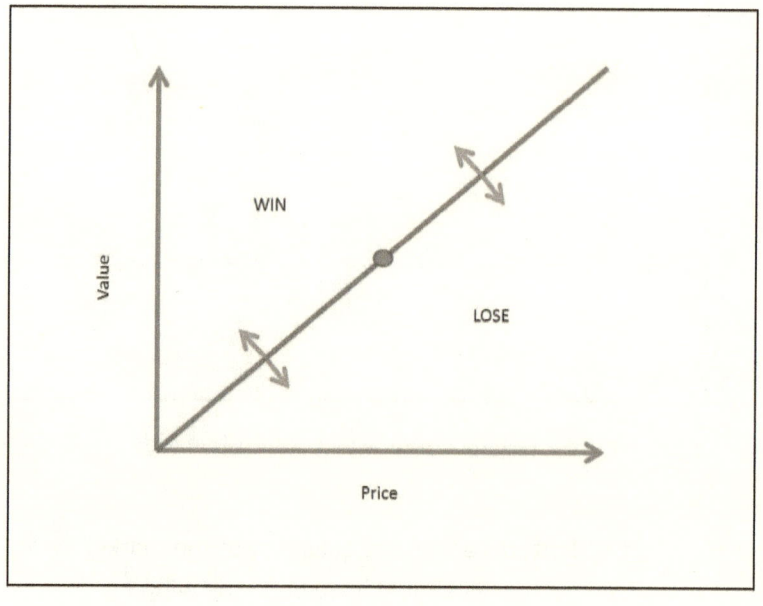

Figure 3 pricing curve showing placement of
winners and losers

Pricing Strategy for Laboratory Instruments

The market value or how much a target market is willing to pay, for your product can be determined by close examination of lost orders. This is actually easier to do if you are not the market leader. The market leader wins most bids providing you with a price and its corresponding feature set. To begin, compile a list of lost orders/bids where you have features that the customer desired and prices provided by you and your competitors. Follow these steps:

1. Tabulate in columns the competitor name and below it the bid price. Be sure and indicate the winning bid. The winning bid will be used as the baseline to gauge which features the customer wants for the winning price.

2. List all the features of the winning bid and those of each competitor.

3. The features and price of the winning
    bid are set as the "neutral point" on a
    price curve similar to Figure 1.

4. Don't forget that "brand name" is a
    psychological feature that could be high
    value to the customer.

5. Find your price and those of non-
    winning competitors on the x axis of the
    price curve.

6. Find your and the competitor's position
    on the line and determine your
    perceived value.

7. If your price was higher than the
    winning price, you cannot trace price all
    the way up to the line; your value
    cannot exceed the perceived value of
    the winning bid.

8. Determine where your price and feature set falls on the value matrix (Figure 4).

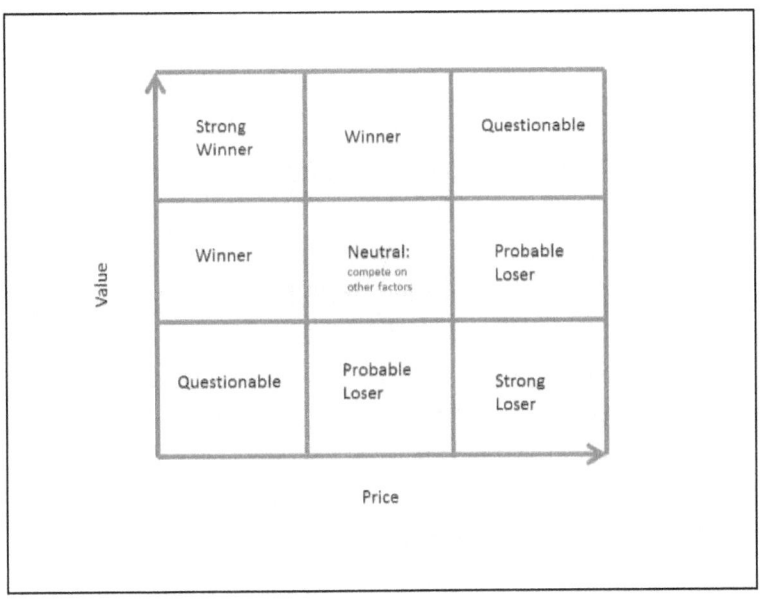

Figure 4 Value matrix

Suppose Company A, Company B, and Company C bid $200,000, $150,000, and $160,000 respectively, on a triple quadrupole GC/MS instrument sale and Company A wins the bid. Plot Company A at $200,000 in the neutral position, trace up vertically to the line, and then trace back to the value. This point is the "value" that the market sees in the Company A feature set for a price of $200,000. Do the same for Company B at $150,000 and Company C at $160,000.   Notice that the market PERCEIVES the value of both Company B and Company C as less than the value of the Company A. Locate S1 on Figure 5. This is client PERCEPTION of the Value/Price of the Company C instrument. Rising to S2 requires communicating to the customer $40,000 extra value just to place Company C equivalent to the customer's PERCEPTION of Company A. Now refer to the Figure 4 Value matrix. Even by raising S1 to S2 (communicating $40,000 of extra value), S2 is still not a "clear winner". More value must be communicated. For example, rising to point S3 adds significant, perhaps even $100,000), more value. Essentially, to overcome the brand recognition of Company A, Company C needed

to communicate about $100,000 extra VALUE. If
marketing communicated VALUE properly,
Company C could have raised their price to
$200,000 and still fall into the winner category
of the value matrix.

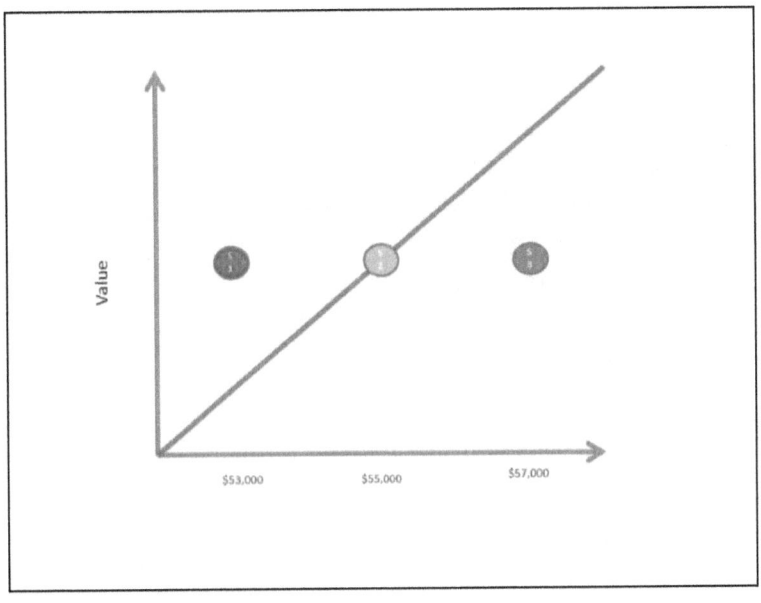

Figure 6 pricing curve with three competitive
bids

For another example, refer to Figure 6. Three prices were quoted for three different competitors all PERCEIVED as having equivalent features/benefits. Also refer to Figure 4 value matrix. S1 is the clear winner, S2 is the market leader (feature set defined by market leader), and S3 is the loser. S1 may have been able to charge $2000 more, however in doing so could have lost to the market leader. S3 needs to either lower their price by $2000 or communicate more value. Unfortunately for S3, vertically tracing S3 to the red line (adding more value) finds S3 still "questionable" on the value matrix.

In this example the customer decided that the market leader's brand was worth approximately $2000.

An analytical approach to calculating economic benefit

Step 1 Define Potential Differentiated Benefits

1. What does the product/feature do?

2. How is the product/feature different from the other alternatives?

   For example, Company A says they have an inert high efficiency self-cleaning source.   How is the Company C's source the same? How is the Company C source different? What are the benefits of the Company C source compared to the Company A? Does the Company C source have:

1. Better sensitivity

2. Reduced cost

3. Less maintenance

4. Reduced sample re-runs

5. Allow you to replace existing
    instruments

Will a new product allow a customer to replace existing products or will it be used in place of existing products? What kind of expertise is necessary to use the Company C product compared to a competitor product? Is it easier, the same, or will it require extensive training?

How much will replacing brand x with a Company C product affect the ENTIRE laboratory operation. Will it disrupt the laboratory or will it improve operations by making everything better. Remember that a laboratory buys an instrument for the results it generates. They may need results from multiple different kinds of instruments / analyses before they can consider all testing complete. How will a new instrument from Company C affect the laboratory's ability to collect data?

Is the new instrument a "game changer"? Is it a whole new way to collect the same type of data, but somehow better?

Step 2 Identify who benefits

Laboratory analysts - less downtime, fewer mistakes, less lab fatigue, less pressure to get things finished, easier to use, larger calibration range, less frequent calibrations

Laboratory management - reduced operating costs, better results, less downtime, less maintenance, rugged, long-term stability

Laboratory QA/QC - fewer QC failures, compliant with method, better records, more traceability, less chance of fraud

Laboratory customer - better results, faster turnaround times, better QA/QC

Step 3 Select the correct metric

For each of the above in Step 2, analyst, manager, QA/QC, or lab customer, it is important to identify the best metric. The metric can vary depending on who your message targets and the message should vary by targeted market. Each target market is segmented and the message can vary per segment. For example, managers of commercial laboratories are concerned with low operational costs and throughput. Managers of non-profit industrial laboratories are less concerned with throughput and more concerned with the correctness of their results.

Step 4 Measure and Quantify

By now you should have a good idea of potential benefits of your instrument/features and who the VALUE is created for. You should also know how each stakeholder will evaluate value.

A test run by a commercial laboratory takes 4 hours, including 1 hour of manual labor, to run 24 samples. The laboratory charges $25 per

sample. The consumable cost per test is $7.00.
Of the 24 samples, 4 are QC for which the
laboratory will not get paid. Assume the labor is
$15.00 per hour. $15.00 times 2.5 = $37.50
takes into account hidden costs and overhead;
actual labor cost is $37.50 per hour.

The cost for the laboratory to rune 24 samples
is:

24 x $7.00 = $168

1 hour labor = $ 37.50

Total = $205.50

Pricing Strategy for Laboratory Instruments

The laboratory invoices

20 x $25 = $500.00

Profit for laboratory = $500 - $205.5 = $294.50

But the laboratory needs to increase capacity. Although they can do 24 tests per 4 hours, in reality, with lunch hour breaks, etc. The laboratory is limited to 24 tests per day maximum in an 8 hour shift. So the laboratory decides to investigate a new technology. The new technology costs $30,000 but is able to process 30 tests in 1 hour with a cost per sample of only $0.50. The laboratory believes they will receive at least double the samples per day, increasing their need to 40 samples per day. This results in 48 tests per day. The

laboratory still intends to charge $25 per test
and still expects a minimum of 1 hour labor. A
comparison of cost is first made at 24 samples:

24 x $0.50 = $12.00

Labor   = $37.50

Total   = $49.50

The laboratory would invoice

20 x 25   = $500

Profit for the laboratory is $450.50 (an increase
of $156)

Based on this analysis, not taking into account increased profit from increased capacity, the laboratory can expect a ~ $3,120 increase in profit per month. Payoff of the new technology comes in about 10 months. However, the laboratory expects to double capacity. This doubling in capacity does not increase the 1 hour labor. Therefore a doubled capacity raises the consumable cost per sample set from $12.00 to $24.00 and the total cost to run 48 samples is $61.50.

The laboratory would invoice

40 x 25   = $1000

Profit for the laboratory is $938.50 (an increase of $644)

Pricing Strategy for
Laboratory Instruments

The laboratory expects the new technology will double their capacity, greatly increase profit for that test, and pay for itself within 3 - 4 months of operation. The laboratory views the technology as low RISK because even if they do not double capacity, they still increase profit and the instrument pays for itself in less than 1 year.

A financial metric may not work for all laboratories. Some may prefer a metric based on improved data quality, or perhaps long-term stability, or lower maintenance.

Pricing Strategy for Laboratory Instruments

Categories of potential value

Category	Example
Operating cost	Efficiency, increased capacity
quality	Data review, re-runs, recalibration,
logistics	Improved turnaround time
technology	Flexibility, future use, new tests
Supplier reliability	Brand dependability, ruggedness, time to service
maintenance	Preventive, downtime
transaction	Ease of purchase

Pricing Strategy for Laboratory Instruments

inventory	Cost of consumables, spare parts
Life cycle costs	Life of product
Opportunity costs	Impact of new instrument/test on entire operation
Asset utilization	Up time
Revenue improvement	New test, throughput
other	Cost of training, ease of use

Example of cost of ownership

Cost	Product A	Product B
Purchase price	$49,000	$54,500
Maintenance (7 years)	$25,000	$18,500
Consumables	$3,000	$1000
Replacement part	$2000	$0
Total Cost of Ownership	$79,000	$74,000

Product B has a higher purchase price, but long-term maintenance is cheaper. Product B provides greater VALUE to the customer.

Factor about product	Benefit to customer	Quantified VALUE
Lower consumable cost	Saves money	$3000-$1000 = $2000
Lower maintenance cost	Saves money	$25,000-$18,500 = $6500
No replacement parts	Saves money	$2000-0 = $2000
TOTAL VALUE		$10,500

Defining a Pricing Strategy

Strategy means to choose who you attempt to sell to and what steps you will take to win. Pricing strategy must be aligned with, and support, the overall marketing strategy. For a

Pricing Strategy for
Laboratory Instruments

pricing strategy to work it must start with a basic understanding of VALUE. This "value" is determined by the customer/target market.

In business to business selling there are a number of inputs used to set price. These include:

1. Cost to manufacture and distribute a product / service

2. What the competition charges for similar products / service

3. Whether the product is distributed, sold direct, or sold on-line

4. The product life cycle

5. VALUE to the customer

Smart pricing strategy begins with asking the right questions.

1. Cost

What is the cost to manufacture, sell, and deliver a product to the customer?

What costs are fixed?

Do costs vary for the various market segments?

Do costs vary geographically?

How will costs change over time?

How do your costs compare with the competitor? (Estimate the competitor at 50% Margin)

2. Channels

Who sells your products?

How will your prices affect them?

3. Competition

Who are your competitors? (Competitors could
be someone selling a similar product, or it could
be anything competing for the same money)

How much do competitors, or competition,
change per target segment?

What are the strengths and weaknesses of your
competition?

4. Value

How do your customers assess value?

How does value vary across markets and market segments?

What level of unmet need exists among the various markets and market segments?

What evidence is needed to substantiate customer value?

5. Company capabilities and goals

What kind of commitment is your company willing to make to generate performance (method) and economic evidence?

What marketing investment is being considered?

How does your company compare to the competitor's marketing, distribution, and service?

6. Product Life Cycle

Where is the product in the technology life cycle?

What is the nature of buyer demand and price sensitivity in the life cycle phase?

Pricing Strategy

Companies should move away from mass marketing and take a targeted marketing approach. Mass marketing assumes that all customers in all markets and all market segments are interested in the same features. In mass marketing, you offer the product to everyone at the same list price. Sales staff discounts in competitive sales situations. Essentially, the customer views the product as a commodity and buys on price. An example of mass marketing is the Ford Model T. All were the same. Another example of mass marketing would be placing an advertisement for diapers in a newspaper. Whoever picks up the newspaper, whether they need diapers or not, see the ad. Money is wasted and the advertiser can expect low returns. Instead, the advertiser for the diapers should place his advertisement in a woman's magazine. Now, only women see the ad. To segment further, the ad is placed in a woman's magazine targeting mothers. This advertiser has just decided to do target marketing. He chose a target market (women) and segmented the market to those women most likely to need diapers. Target marketing assumes that people buy products based on personal preferences, needs, or intended use. Target marketing offers different features, or presents different features differently, to the targeted market depending on perceived needs of the potential customers. Target marketing allows you to price a product based upon its VALUE to the customer. Not all market segments will value a product equally. In target marketing, a company can choose not to market a product to segments that do not perceive a value in the product. Conversely, target marketing allows you to charge a premium for the same product to segments that perceive high value in owning the product.

Decide which markets and which market segments you are going to target and develop a strategy for each segment.

Develop a basic pricing strategy that includes:

1. List Price

2. Target Price (what you expect 80% of market to pay)

3.   Floor Price (the absolute minimum you
     can charge to still breakeven)

If your product is a newly released technology,
or a technology that has never been applied to
the targeted market (perceived by customer as
new technology) you should use a SKIM pricing
strategy. Skim pricing is priced at a very high
margin. Skim pricing is used for innovators and
early adopters who are willing to pay a
premium price to have the newest technology.
When the Apple iPhone was first released,
Apple charged $600 for a new phone with a
phone plan. This was very expensive to a
market used to paying nothing for a new phone
(with a 2 year plan). Early adopters bought the
phone at the high price. Apple then lowered the
price to reach a broader market.

Penetration pricing is often used in attempts to gain market share. Competition will usually respond by also lowering the price. In a fixed size market of mature technology you can only steal share from a competitor. The end result of penetration pricing is price wars, competition on price, and an overall lowering of the market price of the product.

NEUTRAL pricing is setting your price somewhere near the competition and then DECIDING to compete on VALUE.

Demand is derived

Demand for environmental laboratory instruments is determined by regulations and a need for testing. The demand is created by the

number of laboratories and the rate of
replacement of existing instruments. Lowering
the price of a certain value set (instrument) will
not increase the overall market size. The market
size is fixed. Lowering the price may steal some
market share from a competitor for a while.
Eventually, the competitor will respond.

A new technology that replaces an existing one,
a new method that requires a new technology,
or a new technology that automates existing
technologies are ways to CREATE new market
demand. This increases the size of the market.
An example is the analysis of cyanotoxins in
water. If the EPA decides to regulate
cyanotoxins, a demand will require the need for
LCMSMS sales. A new market will come into
being. Its size will be defined by the demand.
Another example is a new method for Total
Nitrogen that could be used to replace TKN, an
older, labor intensive, method. The new TN
method will create a demand for TN analyzers

that did not exist before. The size of this market will be defined by the size of the demand for TN.

Use SKIM pricing when a new demand is created for new method or instrument. For all other cases, in environmental instrument sales, use a neutral pricing strategy that competes on features. These features are communicated to customers as benefits/value. The more value you are able to communicate the higher the price.

Vary Price by Target Market

Prices will vary by target market. But each market has its own maximum and minimum VALUE price based on the benefit of the product's feature set to that particular target market. A "cost-plus" or margin based pricing applies the same price across all markets

despite perceived value by each particular
market. Refer to Figure 7.

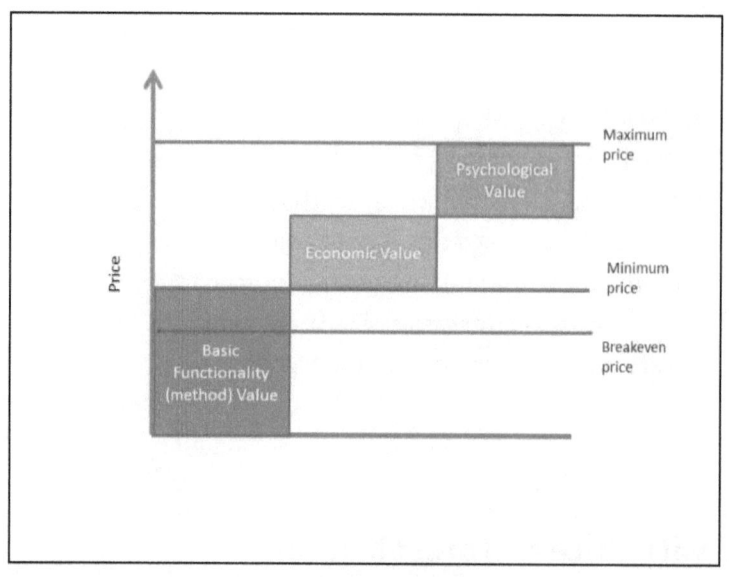

Figure 7 price by value

Pricing Strategy for Laboratory Instruments

Margin pricing determines a cost and multiples by some factor to come up with a breakeven price. Whether doing value pricing or margin pricing, you still want to determine your breakeven price. Never sell below this price. This is where the paths differ. In margin pricing, a maximum margin (for example 70%) is applied to the cost of the product. This becomes the list price. The sales department can now either sell at list price or discount somewhere between break even and list. Value based pricing is somewhat similar to what the salesman does. The salesman evaluates the customer and estimates how much the customer is willing to pay. The salesman starts at list price and works his way down via discounting to the price he thinks the customer will pay. In value pricing there are different list prices depending upon the market and market segment the product is being sold. Products may be bundled differently, or different features highlighted to emphasize value to that market segment. For value pricing to work there needs to be different sets of marketing materials, such as flyers and brochures, specifically mentioning the benefits/features that are of value to those customers. You must also FENCE off other markets so you can price differently across the different markets.

Use fencing so you can charge different markets different prices

Fences enable you to charge different prices to different markets, or charge different prices to different market segments within a market. Fencing needs to be based on objective criteria. An example is how airlines can charge different prices for a different class of seating, or how they can charge different prices for different types of fares. The easiest way to fence off a product is to bundle them specifically for the applications a certain targeted market will do. For example, a GCMS bundle targeted to environmental that includes the instrument, reagents, column, and method could be labeled

the "environmental GCMS". A food testing
customer is not interested in the environmental
bundle and so would not directly compare
pricing of a "pesticide in food" GCMS with an
"environmental" GCMS. Even though these two
"bundles" are the same, they are different to
the customer. Other ways to vary prices
include:

1. Quantity of purchase - if a customer is
   going to buy a lot of the same
   instrument then his price per
   instrument should be lower.

2. Customer Loyalty - If the customer has
   already purchased numerous products
   then reward loyalty.

3. Vary product slightly per market
   segment - offer slightly different
   features to different markets. For
   example, a triple quadrupole GCMS for
   forensics comes with a forensics

database and one for residues in food
may come with a pesticide database.

4. Service needs - different markets may
require different levels of support. For
instance, a university may not need as
rapid a response for service as a
commercial testing laboratory.

How to capture customer value and define units of exchange

1. Price per unit - how much does the
product cost the customer

2. Price per outcome - how much does the
whole purchase, product, service,
consumable, training, warranty cost the
customer.

Even though we tend to think in terms of price per unit, it is the price per outcome that concerns the customer. The customer is investing in capital equipment. Often, particularly since we are not the market leader in most products, the customer is investing in the cost to switch to your company. One way to get a customer to switch (minimize risk) is through service contracts. If you use this approach, be sure to follow the customer's use of the product to ensure you get revenue.

Price Sensitivity Drivers

Operation/results

What is the impact of the product on the customer's results or on his entire laboratory operation? Does the product improve his results? How does the product improve results? How important are these improvements to the customer? Does the product improve (streamline) operations of the laboratory? Did it decrease training needs? Did it decrease consumable or maintenance costs? Is less labor required? Can they get results faster?

If you can clearly communicate better results customers will have lower price sensitivity. Any meaningful, statistically significant improvement will have greater value. An example is the decrease in run time possible using the fast scanning capability of a modern GCMS. In itself, fast scanning is a meaningless feature to the average customer. However, by collecting data that shows equivalent performance for EPA Method 8270 at a 15 minute run time compared to a 30 minute runtime you can communicate value. The 30 minute run time only allows a customer to analyze 24 samples per 12 hour tune window. A

15 minute run time allows the customer to run twice as many samples in the same amount of time. A pay per test laboratory would find great value in this. This benefit of the fast scanning feature greatly increases value and lowers price sensitivity.

An unmet need could be ease of use for a hard to run alternative. Other unmet needs could be a new instrument required for compliance with a new regulation, or a new way to do an existing test that is better compared to other ways. A simple, new way to run Total Nitrogen compared to TKN plus nitrate/nitrite fits the criteria for an unmet need. This new method, when approved, will create a demand for a TOC analyzer with a TN module. Since the method is easier and faster than the existing method it has low price sensitivity.

Perceived risk

Buyers are the most price sensitive when they perceive a risk of not being able to achieve the same outcome as they do (or will) with the market leader. The non-market leader must always offer a COMPELLING reason, such as PROVABLE productivity benefits and labor savings. Without compelling evidence the customer is price sensitive. This forces you to discount. Similar is the perceived purchase risk. "No one ever gets fired for buying the market leader". You must overcome this fear, or you will be forced to lower price.

References and fairness

Value and price are perceived. Buyers perceive value through a human lens. The corresponding price must be fair compared to a reference.

Pricing Strategy for Laboratory Instruments

Most likely this reference will be the market leader's price and feature set. The reference could also be a previous purchase made by the customer on the older product you are replacing.

Strategy is about choice. Pricing strategy is the choice made for pricing each product per target segment/market. Value, as perceived by the target customer, should be the foundation of your pricing strategy.

Developing an Offering Strategy

An offering strategy enables you to serve
different target markets and make a profit.
Target markets vary by:

- Needs

- Behavior

- Willingness to pay

- Cost to serve

You must vary your offering to take into
account the differences between the target
markets. With a single offering there is no way
to vary the value offered to a customer. This

gives you very little flexibility, other than discounting, to meet customer needs. With a flexible offering you can trade value for price.

You can vary the following to create different offerings:

1. Core product

2. Support services

3. Business terms of transaction

Always provide customers with three product offerings and set the offerings priced at one of the following ratios:

A. 12:20:60

B. 3:5:15

C. 1:2:4

This process, called "anchoring" encourages the customer to compare your product with your other similar products instead of to a competitor.

The anchor price is a fully loaded, feature packed very high priced version of the product. You do not really expect to sell many of these. The purpose is to make the mid-priced product seem like a better deal.

The lower priced product is feature shy and priced so close to the middle product that the customer will choose the middle product.

The mid-priced product is the one you expect and are intending to sell to that particular target.

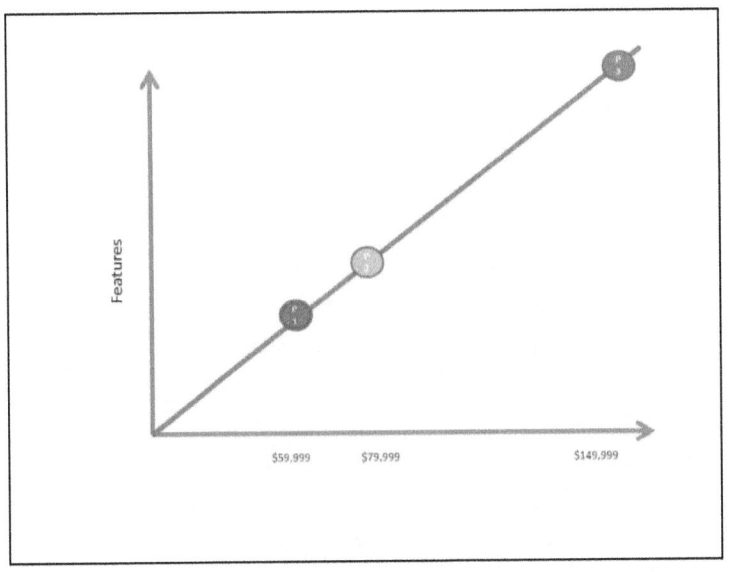

Figure 8 Offering Strategy

For example see Figure 8:

1. Option P1 = $59,999, a single
    quadrupole GCMS with slower scan

speed, less sensitivity, and a small
vacuum pump

2. Option P2 = $79,999, a single
   quadrupole GCMS with rapid scan
   speed capable of doubling throughput
   compared to P1, 5 - 10 times the
   sensitivity of P1, and a much faster
   pump down with lower noise than p1

3. Option P3 = $149,999, a triple
   quadrupole with the same features as
   P2 plus the ability to do MRM.
   However, this customer is only seeking
   single quadrupole instruments.

In the example, Option P1 is missing a key some
time-saving feature/benefits.   Option P2 has
the time-saving feature/benefit. The individual
price of the key time-saving feature/benefits
exceeds the $20,000 difference between Option

P1 and Option P2. The customer chooses Option P2.

Option P3 makes Option P2 not seem so expensive.

With only one option, a customer will tend to start comparing features to those of a competitor. Ideally, your options are bundled with one price per bundle and the customer has no visibility of the price of individual components/features. This makes it harder to make feature to feature comparisons with a competitor product.

Drivers of profitability

Set prices that capture premium value. Recognize that different markets and different market segments have different price sensitivities and willingness to pay. Always drive your customers to your most profitable products. (Assuming the product does the method/ fits the need) Minimize discounts and charge for service visits. Reduce the cost to serve. Avoid demos and running customer samples unless you know that success will result in a sale. Be sure the demo does not cost more than your profit. Eliminate, or minimize "freebies" just to close a deal. Cross-sell different product to the same customer. The goal is to make a profit. For most products, environmental is a mature market. In a mature market, customers view laboratory instruments as a commodity. Sell on value. Discounting is a losing strategy.

Most environmental customers have been conditioned to negotiate pricing and expect some sort of discount. Before we continue, let's review:

Pricing Strategy for Laboratory Instruments

We already know our target market and the individually targeted market segments. There needs to be an offering strategy for each segment and a target price level for each instrument. The target price is somewhere between the list price and the minimum price (see Figure 7). There must be price fences, preferably environmentally named bundled "packages" to prevent other market segments from comparing price. Any discounting strategy must consider:

1. Value and willingness to pay

2. Cost to serve

3. Purchasing volume

4. Related purchases

5. Ability of this particular customer to influence others

The discounting structure needs to be logical, defensible, aligned with cost to serve, and able to drive the right customer behavior.

It is possible to "map" out a discount prioritizing scheme. In our example, we will use four weighted criteria and use them to drive discounting.

Criteria	Range (low discount to high discount)	Weight (%)
Purchasing value of the customer	1 - 10	40
Ability of this customer to control the purchase	1 - 10	40

Pricing Strategy for Laboratory Instruments

Strategic importance of this customer to target segment	1 - 10	10
Relative cost to serve this customer	1 - 10	10

For an example we will use a $5M per year commercial laboratory located in Wyoming. The manager of the laboratory is an officer in ASTM, innovates new methods, and has written at least one EPA method. The laboratory buys new instruments and does not have a psychological attachment to the market leader. The number of instruments is low relative to a larger commercial lab. The laboratory is remote, however, resulting in a high cost to serve. Based on this description of this lab, the following factors were calculated. Purchasing power (5 x 0.4) 2, Ability to control the purchase (8 x 0.4) 3.6, Strategic importance to the targeted

segment (10 x 0.1) 1, Cost to serve (1 x 0.1) 0.1.
The total discount priority factor = 6.7.
Therefore, this customer is determined to
receive a small discount.

Using this strategy calculates the following
prioritization of discounting to the average of
the following indicated market segments:

Industrial (5) < small commercial (5-6) <
Municipal laboratories (7) < large commercial
laboratories (8)

1. Discounting cheapens the
   product/brand. If necessary, replace the
   discount with "buy one and get the
   other at a lower price". Buy one at full
   price; buy one at a lower price does not

cause customers to think it is a cheap
product.

2. Discounting, unless it is made plain that
    the discount is temporary and a sound
    reason is given for the discount
    (refurbished inventory, etc.), causes the
    customer to always be waiting for the
    next discount.   Think Jos. A Banks "buy
    one get two free". Ever buy at full price
    at Jos A. Banks?

    a. Ever wonder how much
        discounting affects the "bottom
        line"?

    b. A 20% discount off of a 55% GM
        list price means you have to sell
        3 to get the same profit you
        would have made from selling 2
        at the list price.

    c. A 20% discount off of a 40% GM
        list price means you have to sell

2 to get the same profit you would have made from selling 1 at the list price.

d. A 20% discount off of a 25% GM list price means you have to sell 4 to get the same profit you would have made from selling 1 at the list price

Set prices based on value. However, the value must be communicated. And VALUE IS PERCEIVED by the customer. You must have the right messaging, tools, and evidence so the customer can know value. Value is expressed in monetary and laboratory method terms. Value is what the customer receives in return for what he has paid. Raising or lowering your price does not change the products value. Changing the price only changes the buyer's incentive. At a given price (market value) the seller who exceeds at communicating value wins. This value is relative to competing alternatives and

prices. One alternative is always status quo. The
actual value is quantifiable:

1. Samples per hour

2. Cost per sample

3. Detection limit

4. Calibration range

5. Calibration frequency

6. Signal drift over time

7. Maintenance costs

8. Consumable costs

9. Downtime

10. Number of repeat tests due to off scale
    peaks or QC failures

11. Recovery on certified reference materials

12. Accuracy and precision in real matrices similar to what the customer runs

13. Psychological value (aka "will I get fired?")

Benefit Communication

Guarantees and risk sharing can help to overcome the psychological barriers. Once overcome and the customer is willing to objectively evaluate the instrument, you need to communicate method performance and economic benefits. Economic benefits are the ones that laboratory managers and purchasing agents will use to decide. Laboratory managers and purchasing will be concerned with the disruption that a new product, particularly not the market leader, will cause to the entire operation. This disruption will become the main sales objection once ability of the instrument/product to meet all method requirements has been established. Sales presentations need to assure the customer that disruption will be minimal. To do this, the sales person needs to understand the laboratory's operation (whether a commercial lab that cannot afford to wait to be trained or a municipal/industrial lab that needs to do permit work).

Communicating economic benefit requires usable value selling tools. Some of these may be flyers, brochures, and a web-site. However, the more expensive the product becomes the more the need for complex, very specific data driven documents with believable, measurable criteria. To complete a complex sale, there needs to be an abundant supply of application notes written using the exact methods on similar matrices that the customer is interested in. Preferably, the sales person has access to several references or testimonials made by users familiar with the instrument and the tests the customer plans to do. Hopefully, before the potential sale comes to the necessity of presenting this type of information the sales process has been followed and the customer is ready to buy. Unfortunately, 43% of companies do not even have a formal sales process. Without a sales process implementation of value selling tools is very difficult.

Summary of Pricing Strategy

The previous sections described a pricing strategy that can be used to sell complex laboratory instruments. Emphasis was made on the environmental market segment. The strategy can be applied across all market segments. For pricing strategy to be effective there must be an established sales process. The sales process is especially important to control the dissemination of information as the value of products is communicated. The most difficult value to overcome is the psychological value that the market applies to the market leader. Once the psychological objection is overcome, a premium price can be made based on economic value of the instrument. This strategy bases pricing and feature sets on the price and features of the market leader.

Marketing and the Sales Process

Marketing efforts are measured by the total opportunity generated and quantified in financial terms. Marketing efforts judged by lead creation alone do not accurately reflect the leads that resulted in sales. For example, it is possible to generate 1000 leads and get one sale. Or it is possible to generate 100 leads and get 10 sales. Obviously 10 sales is better. Thus, you quantify the marketing strategy not by the number of leads, but by an increase in sales.

How to generate leads

Lead generation is the most important objective of business-to-business marketing. There is no point in "branding", creating great application notes, attending trade shows, or even placing an ad if these activities do not generate high quality leads. A scientific organization may feel they are "transferring scientific knowledge", but without sales there is no reason for the organization to exist. Without leads, there can be few sales.

A lead is a prospect who has expressed INTEREST in buying something. A list of names of trade show attendees are not leads. Inquiries may be future leads for nurturing by marketing. Do not transfer inquiries to sales.

Lead generation consists of a series of steps. A person does not go from "I saw your logo" to "I want to buy". Marketing generates the first inquiry and guides it to a sale.

Marketing maintains "ownership" of the inquiry and nurtures potential customers with a steady stream of information until they are ready to buy. The sales process and marketing must be intertwined. It is marketing's job to look at the product from a third person perspective. How does the customer perceive the product? What is the customer's interaction with the product and/or company like? Does the company and/or do the products make the customer's life easier?

The customer sees you through:

1. Advertising

2. How you answer the phone

3. How you perform service

Pricing Strategy for Laboratory Instruments

4. Your web-site

5. Trade shows

6. Networking

7. Word of mouth

8. Direct mail

9. Newsletters

10. Public relations

11. Logo

12. Packaging

13. Point of Sale

14. E-mails

15. Proposals

16. Invoices

17. Public presentations

18. Employees

19. Products

Everything the customer hears, sees, reads, and touches before and after a sale affects the customer's perception of your company.

Lead generation relies on direct marketing with specific goals that expect a specific action. The action could be a "click" to register for a seminar or to download a whitepaper. Until the customer is ready to buy, the marketing piece should not expect the action to be "click here to place an order".

Lead generation is about QUALITY not quantity. You want targeting. The tighter the target the higher the response will be. Each specific e-mail should have a specific offer. The offer MOTIVATES the next action. Most business-to-business inquiries ask for more information. The fulfillment content should match the need and

provide VALUE. Do not simply answer an
enquiry with a general brochure! A business
buyer does research long before they are ready
to buy. The business buyer must be MOTIVATED
with content that educates, informs, and
creates DESIRE. The content must speak directly
to the buyer. Content must address the buyers
specific needs and be targeted to his specific
market.

Internal Marketing is also important. The
company's brand and purpose must be clear
and something employees want to be a part of.

Marketing is creating and keeping customers. It
involves "pull" marketing and "push"
marketing. Pull marketing creates a demand
through advertising, oral presentations,
webinars, word of mouth, etc., and push

marketing is direct selling, prospecting, trade
shows, e-mail blasts, direct mail, etc.

The world is not a market

There are at least two main approaches to
marketing. One approach is product marketing
(or mass marketing) and the other is target
marketing.

Product marketing focuses on features and
assumes all customers care about the same
features equally. Product marketing treats the
product as a commodity. If a customer
perceives a product as a commodity he sees all
features of equal value and competition is by
price.

Target marketing focuses on the needs of defined customer sets and emphasizes benefits that those customers will perceive as most valuable. Different customer segments may perceive different value for the same product features. Target marketing enables premium pricing based on perceived value.

Vertical marketing is another term for target marketing. Horizontal marketing is another term for product (or mass) marketing. Vertical marketing caters to the specific needs of specific industries. Horizontal marketing presents features equally to all customers regardless of their intended use of the product. Below is an example of vertical and horizontal marketing.

Pricing Strategy for Laboratory Instruments

Product	Market Product Mix			
	Environmental	Food	Energy	Pharmaceutical
ICP	Yes (EPA methods)	yes	yes	yes
AA	Yes (EPA methods)	yes	yes	no
UV-Vis	Yes (Standard Methods)	Yes (AOAC)	yes	yes
GC	yes(GC-ECD, FPD, NPD)(EPA)	yes(GC-ECD, FPD, NPD)(AOAC)	Yes (system GC FID, TCD)(ASTM)	Yes
GCMS	Yes (single quadrupole) (EPA)	Yes (triple quadru	maybe	maybe

		pole) (AOAC)		
LC	Yes (IC) (EPA)	Yes (AOAC)	Yes (bioethanol)	Yes (company specific)
LCMS	Yes (cyanotoxins) (EPA)	Yes (AOAC)	no	Yes
X-Ray	no	Yes (metals)	Yes (sulfur and halogens)	Yes (metals)
TOC	yes	no	no	Yes (CIP)
TN	yes	no	no	no

This marketing mix is an example. It may not be completely accurate for the market segments. The purpose of this example is to illustrate that

not all products apply equally to all markets.
Some markets may not have a market in certain
segments. For instance, there is not much need
for determination of total nitrogen in aqueous
solutions in the food market, and there is little
or no demand for X-Ray in environmental
testing. Also, note that the usage of the
instrument varies per market. GC is a good
example. Environmental and food both need GC
for the analysis of specific pesticides, however,
environmental requires EPA methods and food
requires AOAC methods. Customers looking for
a GC to analyze trace pesticides in water will
not be swayed by advertisements/brochures
emphasizing the analysis of pesticides in
produce. The petrochemical industry is not
interested in GC for pesticide analysis at all.
Instead, they are interested in simulated
distillation and analysis of hydrocarbons.
Targeted marketing provides customers with
information about the product that applies only
to his specific needs.

Pricing Strategy for
Laboratory Instruments

The traditional sales process does not work when selling to scientists. The traditional process is to create some kind of interest for the product, and then create a desire for the product, and then ask for the order. A traditional sale is invasive meaning that sales or marketing pushes information to a potential customer whether he wants it or not. Scientists prefer to do their own investigations; scientists think differently than the mass market.

Scientists must first believe that they have a need for the test that the instrument does, or that they need a new instrument that will enable them to do the test better. Then they will investigate, on their own, using whatever resources are available. The scientist will search the web, go to trade shows, download and read peer reviewed and other technical articles, and ask his peers. Only after the scientists gathers about 80% of the information he needs to make

a decision will he be interested in calling a
company to request more information. Your
publicly available information needs to speak
specifically to the scientists needs. He must be
able to view your information and it be clear
enough for him to deduce on his own that your
instruments are suitable for his intended
purpose. This information cannot be product
specifications. It cannot be features. The
information readily available must be use of our
instruments in running samples similar to what
the scientist will run. The information must
speak of the BENEFITS of using your instrument
compared to other options. The information
must speak of benefits important to the
scientist's specific market segment. For
example, some may be interested in throughput
and some not care about throughput at all.

Barriers to selling to scientists are rarely price.
Instead, the barriers consist of a need to PROVE
to the scientist that the instrument works for

what he needs it to do. The following table is an
example of some of the barriers in each of the
information gathering phases the scientist may
go through.

Pricing Strategy for Laboratory Instruments

Recognition of a need	Exploration of all data pertaining to the technology	Evaluation of specific technology / instruments
Brand awareness	Credibility of the data presented	Credibility of the data presented
Budgets	Peer validation	Sales coverage
Competitive noise	References	Demo variability
Unique/proprietary products	Commodity status	Availability of service

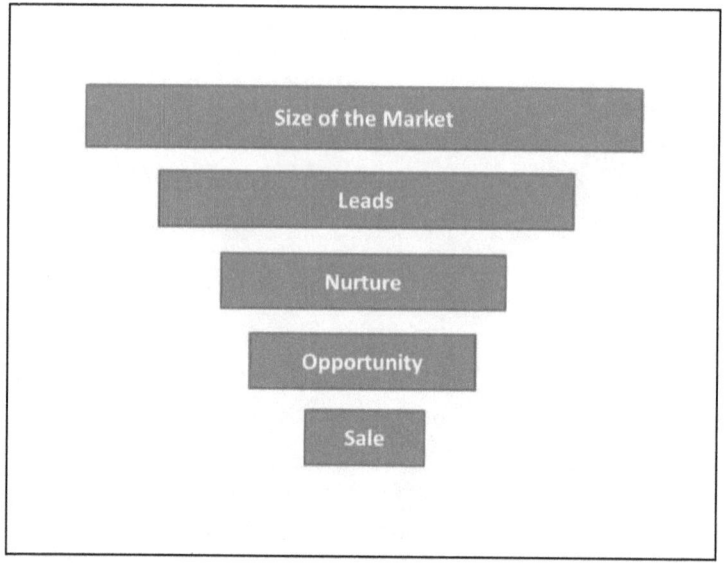

Figure 9 sales funnel

It is important to understand the barriers
scientists discover as they embark on their
journey of recognition, exploration, and
evaluation of new products. It is marketing's
role to ensure that everything the scientists

86

sees, hears, reads, or touches establishes a
need or reinforces value of the product.
Marketing must fully explain the benefits/value
of product features and create a desire to buy.
Refer to Figure 9 Sales Funnel. Marketing's role
is not only to get leads, but also to nurture the
leads, convert them to opportunities, and then
help ensure the opportunities result in sales.
When marketing to scientists the content is
king. The better the content (information made
available to the scientist during the recognition
and exploration phase) the higher the
conversion rate from lead to opportunity and
from opportunity to sale.

Educational content supports your core claim
about an instrument. If you say your instrument
is capable of running EPA Method 624, then you
need to have readily accessible data
demonstrating the instrument running method
624. The content must show analyses being run
in a manner similar to the requirements of the

potential customer. Environmental laboratories are highly regulated and required to follow strict quality assurance/quality control (QA/QC) protocols. Data must demonstrate that the QA/QC was followed and data must include real world samples and/or reference materials. Environmental laboratory scientists are not interested in how well an instrument performs on standards; they are only interested in real samples.

Environmental scientists do not trust universities. College professors and their students are not highly regulated, do not have to follow strict QA/QC, and often modify methods without sufficient explanation as to why the method was modified. Environmental scientists expect the instrument manufacturer to be the expert at his own instruments, and so therefore, expect the instrument manufacturer to collect and present their own data.

Pricing Strategy for Laboratory Instruments

Environmental scientists are interested in content that establishes leadership by challenging existing methods and proving that there are suitable alternatives. Environmental scientists turn to manufacturers that work with EPA and consensus organizations that develop new methods designed to save time and money. Always challenging the status quo establishes your company as an expert.

Persuasive content includes putting the scientist in direct contact with the instrument. This includes demos, peer references, and analysis of customer samples.

Sales campaign should disseminate information slowly and in accordance to the phase that the customer is in at that time. If the customer is still in the recognition phase you would not want to send him a feature rich brochure or specification sheet. Below is an example of the types of marketing material a customer should receive in the phases of recognition, exploration, and evaluation.

Pricing Strategy for
Laboratory Instruments

Phase	Recognition	Exploration	Evaluation
Content	Leadership	Educational	Persuasive
Typical examples	Social media	Social media	promotions
	White papers	White papers / articles	endorsements
	Conference presentations	On-line tutorials	Sales support
	Advertising	Web site	Sales demo
	Direct Mail	User groups	Application notes
	Giveaways	Vendor newsletter	Technical support documentation

Pricing Strategy for Laboratory Instruments

	Trade Show	webinars	Product brochure
	General brochure	Information booklets	Instrument specifications
	Press releases		

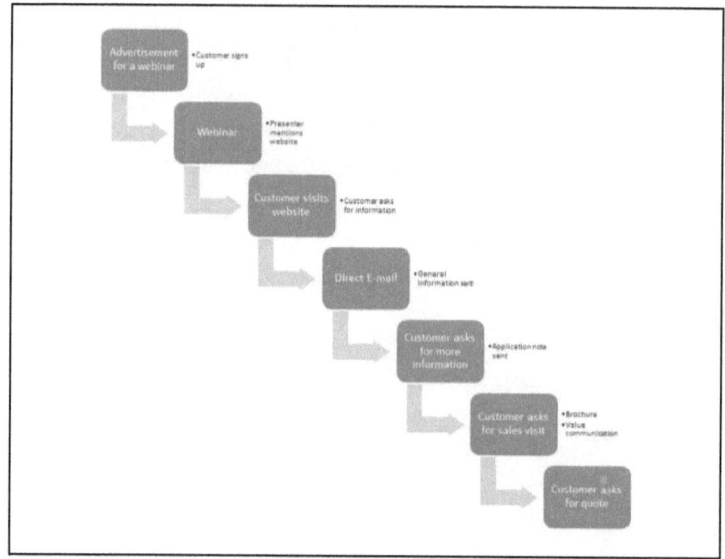

Figure 11 content roadmap

Figure 11 is an example of a content road map. In this example a potential customer signs up for a webinar. During the webinar, the presenter mentions the company web site. The potential customer visits the company web site and clicks a link asking for information. The information is downloaded and a direct e-mail

92

is sent acknowledging the download.   The
customer responds to the e-mail asking for
more specific information.   An application
note is sent. The customer contacts the
company again asking for more information and
for sales to visit. The sales person visits the
customer, and using the product brochure
explains the features of the instrument
emphasizing the benefits specific to that
customer's market. The customer perceives
value in the product and asks for a quote.
Figure 11 is just an example of one possible
road map to disseminate information to the
customer.

Conclusion

This brief document described a potential pricing Strategy for Laboratory Instruments and Marketing and Sales Process. Examples used, and the processes themselves were based upon research conducted by the author. Emphasis was made on the environmental market. The strategy should apply to all market segments.